INDIGENOUS
PEOPLES' RIGHTS

Indigenous
Peoples' Rights

BY KATIE MARSICO

Content Consultant
C. Richard King,
professor and chair of the Department of Comparative Ethnic Studies
Washington State University

ABDO
Publishing Company

CREDITS

Published by ABDO Publishing Company, 8000 West 78th Street, Edina, Minnesota 55439. Copyright © 2012 by Abdo Consulting Group, Inc. International copyrights reserved in all countries. No part of this book may be reproduced in any form without written permission from the publisher. The Essential Library™ is a trademark and logo of ABDO Publishing Company.

Printed in the United States of America, North Mankato, Minnesota
062011
092011

 THIS BOOK CONTAINS AT LEAST 10% RECYCLED MATERIALS.

Editor: Amy Van Zee
Copy Editor: Sarah Beckman
Interior Design and Production: Kazuko Collins
Cover Design: Marie Tupy

Library of Congress Cataloging-in-Publication Data
Marsico, Katie, 1980-
  Indigenous peoples' rights / by Katie Marsico.
    p. cm. -- (Essential issues)
  Includes bibliographical references and index.
  ISBN 978-1-61783-135-5
  1. Indigenous peoples--Civil rights. I. Title.
  JZ4974.M37 2012
  323.11--dc22
                                        2011009540

TABLE OF CONTENTS

Chief Looking Horse of South Dakota's Lakota Tribe, right, attends a United Nations conference in 2001.

LIFE ON A LAKOTA RESERVATION

In September 2009, 54-year-old Herbert Hale had no electricity or running water. A member of the Lakota tribe, he lived in a one-room house on the Cheyenne River Reservation in Cherry Creek, South Dakota. A feature story by

Cable News Network (CNN) drew attention to his situation. Though Hale was suffering from a brain tumor, he was still the primary caregiver for his diabetic sister. This task was not made any easier by his limited income. He reported taking whatever odd jobs he could find. Hale received checks from a tribal welfare fund that paid him approximately $17 a week.

Hale faced a large problem: a lack of employment opportunities in Cherry Creek. This dilemma is common on many reservations, which are areas the US government has set aside for use by Native Americans. Over the last several centuries, officials who were determined to expand US borders pushed tribes off the lands that once belonged to their tribal ancestors.

In most situations, Native Americans were barely compensated for this land. They were forced onto western reservations that lacked decent farmland and other necessary resources. Even after living in these areas for several years, numerous tribes continue to live in poverty. However, many choose to remain on

The Lakota

Who exactly are the Lakota? These indigenous people belong to a confederation, or alliance, of seven Sioux tribes. Many experts believe that the Lakota have been in North America for several hundred years. Much of the tribe currently lives on reservations in South Dakota. A recent study revealed that more than 50 percent of Lakota families live below the poverty line, versus 9.2 percent of the total number of families who live in South Dakota.

the reservations. They are places for them to practice and celebrate their cultural traditions as a larger community.

For Hale and others like him, life is a cycle of economic hardship. He described routinely traveling to Eagle Butte, South Dakota, to hunt for any work that might earn him a few dollars. Eagle Butte is located approximately 40 miles (64 km) from Cherry Creek. Hale often traveled on foot because he was not able to afford a car. He admitted to CNN:

> *Sometimes it's a long walk, especially in February. Twenty [degrees] below [zero] and I have to walk. . . . A few times I felt like falling asleep on the road. I told myself, "Fall asleep, you're froze and you're gone." I pushed myself to keep walking.*[1]

Stories such as Hale's are common on Native American reservations throughout the United States. Cherry Creek serves as an example of the challenges faced by the nation's indigenous peoples.

In 2009, more than 80 percent of the population on Hale's reservation were unemployed. A little less than 56 percent of the residents in his county are living below the poverty line. For children in the county, the poverty rate is at 70 percent. That same year, officials representing the Lakota tribe shared their observations about their situation. "I feel that we are forgotten because we don't have that voice out there," one chairman explained. "It's demoralizing in a way for some of our members that go out and receive an education and come back and are unable to get a job here."[2]

Another local leader emphasized that the reservation's poverty was rooted in public misunderstanding and limited political representation. "When it comes down to a vote, a lot of the urban representatives, I don't think

Languages or Cultural Legacies?

One critical issue that affects indigenous peoples is the preservation of their languages. The way native groups speak reflects their heritage. Oral histories are passed on through the generations. In addition, songs in native languages are used in ceremonies and hold special meaning.

However, as indigenous peoples blend into mainstream society, they often adopt the language used by that culture. For example, having been schooled in English, many Native Americans now speak English instead of their traditional tongues.

Native American leaders believe that their languages are in danger of disappearing completely if greater efforts are not taken to incorporate them into day-to-day life. Lakota is one language at risk. One group, the Lakota Language Consortium (LLC), wants to make resources available so every Lakota child can become proficient in the language. The group has developed language materials for students, and more than 5,000 students in North and South Dakota participate in the LLC's programs.

Lakota chiefs gather at the Pine Ridge Indian Reservation in South Dakota. This reservation has a population of approximately 40,000.

they really know the plight on the reservation," he remarked. "I think there is a stereotype out there that all tribes have casinos and that's not true."[3]

Yet stereotypes and discrimination do not just affect Native Americans. These forms of social inequality impact indigenous peoples all over the globe. Injustices relating to economics, land rights, and cultural preservation also impact these groups. Their struggles—and society's solutions to them—are viewed as essential issues in the twenty-first century.

DEFINING INDIGENOUS PEOPLES

From African Bushmen to Native American tribes such as the Lakota, approximately 370 million indigenous peoples resided in an estimated 90 countries in 2006. These people make up approximately 5 percent of the world population. Indigenous peoples are sometimes called aboriginals or natives. In other instances, they are referred to as first peoples or autochthonous peoples. They belong to ethnic groups that have the earliest known connections to certain geographic regions. In many cases, they are linked to cultures that date back tens of thousands of years.

Worldwide organizations such as the United Nations (UN), the World Bank (WB), and the International Labour Organization (ILO) have developed additional criteria to describe indigenous populations. Indigenous groups have existed in a

The Maori

The Maori are a people group of New Zealand. Scientists believe the Maori were the first people of New Zealand, arriving around 1300 CE or earlier.

The first European contact occurred in the 1600s. In the following centuries, Europeans continued to come to the area. Diseases, weapons, and new ways of life began to threaten the Maori. They engaged in many battles to defend their land against the British who began populating the island.

The struggle for land and cultural preservation is a goal that continues today, and important steps have been made. The Maori play a large role in New Zealand's government, where seven of the 120 seats in Parliament are reserved for the Maori. In 1987, the Maori language became an official language of the nation.

particular area before it was colonized or annexed by outside foreign powers. Indigenous peoples maintain cultural differences that distinguish them from the mainstream societies that surround them. Finally, these individuals either identify themselves as being indigenous or are recognized this way by other groups.

Their far-reaching history in a certain region or country does not mean that indigenous peoples are always treated with respect or social awareness. Their cultures are often at odds with mainstream values and institutions. Their methods of survival and their traditional attitudes do not always fit into the fast-paced worlds of industry and technology around them.

In addition, they generally do not enjoy the same political or social representation as other ethnic groups. As a result, indigenous peoples often must fight to overcome poverty and preserve their lands and ways of life. Many of these individuals face the difficult choice of assimilating into, or blending in

Population Statistics

In 2005, population numbers for indigenous peoples were listed at approximately 370 million. However, estimates are hard to obtain. There are many different standards used to qualify the term *indigenous peoples*. These range from a group's political standing to its pattern of cultural or technological development. In addition, these individuals often live in remote regions or have begun to blend in with mainstream society. These patterns affect official censuses.

with, mainstream cultures. Or they might deal with discrimination as they attempt to protect their own.

Growing numbers of world citizens refuse to accept that indigenous peoples should be limited to following one of these two pathways in the twenty-first century. Organizations and legislation aim to further the rights of these groups. Advocates of indigenous peoples frequently support fair trade as well.

Addressing Issues Indigenous Peoples Face

Fair trade is a market philosophy. The practice is designed to help producers in developing nations achieve economic independence. Fair trade advocates believe that these producers should be paid competitive market prices. In return, these producers are expected to reinvest in their businesses. This helps benefit the larger community. Fair trade is also based on labor standards that guarantee workers' rights. Production methods that are respectful of the environment are also a large part of the fair trade model.

Advocates of fair trade argue that it allows indigenous peoples to produce and create items according to their own specific cultural practices.

**International Day
of the World's
Indigenous People**

In December 1994, the
UN named August 9
the International Day of
the World's Indigenous
People. As former UN
Secretary General Kofi
Annan explained, "This
commemoration is an
opportunity to celebrate
the richness of indigenous
cultures and the contri-
butions of indigenous
peoples to the human
family. But more impor-
tantly, it is a chance for
men and women every-
where to take stock of the
situation of indigenous
peoples in our world
today, and of how much
more needs to be done to
improve their lives."[4]

They believe that it preserves the heritage of these groups by enabling them to earn income and build stable, self-sufficient communities. But not everyone agrees that fair trade is an effective way to aid indigenous peoples. Opponents of this market system insist that it is more successful in making consumers feel socially responsible than it is in actually helping the world's poorest people. Nevertheless, fair trade is one example of how society is searching for solutions.

Another important approach is to increase education about indigenous peoples. Their unique backgrounds reflect some of the earliest civilizations on Earth. The issues that threaten their cultural survival include topics ranging from human rights to economic equality. World citizens have different opinions about how to protect indigenous groups. However, the majority agrees that it is crucial that the unique diversity of indigenous peoples continues in centuries to come.

Buks, 45, belongs to a clan that is part of Africa's Bushmen.

*Many African Bushmen still use traps, bows and arrows,
or spears to hunt game.*

FROM SOUTHERN AFRICA TO INDIA

Indigenous peoples across the globe share common challenges and are at the center of a variety of current issues and debates. The more well known of these groups include Africa's Bushmen, Australia's Aborigines, and Asia's Adivasis.

The Bushmen, who are also commonly referred to as San, were southern Africa's earliest inhabitants. They are also sometimes called Sho, Basarwa, !Kung, or Khwe. These people are traditionally hunter-gatherers. Experts believe they have populated the area for perhaps tens of thousands of years. Early Bushmen were nomadic. They traveled from place to place within their territories. While some hunted game, others collected food such as berries, roots, and melons.

Yet life for the Bushmen was not all about survival. The Bushmen are skilled artists. Their paintings of nature can be found in caves and on rocks throughout southern Africa. Their art tells the stories of their spiritual beliefs and reveals their rituals.

Today, approximately 100,000 Bushmen live in Botswana, South Africa, Namibia, and Angola. Their culture is seriously threatened. Toward the start of the twentieth century, Europeans colonizing portions of the continent clashed with the indigenous peoples living there. The Bushmen were often killed or enslaved. They were forced to largely abandon their lifestyle as hunter-gatherers. Many are now farmers, but few are successful.

The Bushmen are also struggling to cope with modern issues. These range from human immunodeficiency virus (HIV) to teen pregnancy to the inability to find work. Local governments have attempted to push the Bushmen off their lands to develop property or to encourage large-scale farming or mining efforts. Eighty-four-year-old Bushman Monto Masako expressed his despair when he was interviewed in 2007. "I feel caged," he remarked. "My father taught me to hunt with a bow and arrow. We slept in the veld [open grasslands]—it was so free. But that has all been taken away, we can never go back."[1]

Indigenous Australians

Similar inequality occurs all over the globe, including in Australia. Indigenous peoples who occupy the Australian mainland and nearby islands are often referred to as Aborigines. Some experts guess they have resided there for approximately 70,000 years. Specific groups now prefer to be called by more distinct names based on their individual tribal identities and locations. Others would rather be described simply as indigenous Australians.

Dance, music, and singing are important forms of expression in Australian Aboriginal culture.

In 2006, Australia was home to approximately 460,000 Aborigines. At the time, this represented 2 percent of Australia's total population. Before the British began colonizing the continent in the late eighteenth century, the Aborigines were mainly hunter-gatherers. Their population included approximately 250 indigenous nations and just as many languages.

European colonization also meant new diseases and a loss of land for the Aborigines. Certain groups were wiped out by very contagious infections such as smallpox. Meanwhile, the British cleared lands that had previously been used for aboriginal hunting and used them for farming and other development. In the centuries that followed, a large number of Australia's indigenous peoples began blending into European culture. They worked on cattle and sheep stations and served in both World War I (1914–1918) and World War II (1939–1945).

From the mid-1900s onward, Aborigines have pushed to maintain their rights and cultural heritage. A large percentage now lives alongside other ethnic groups in Australia's urban settings. However,

Australia's Stolen Generations

Some Australians look back in sorrow on what are referred to as their nation's "stolen generations."[2] This term refers to the approximately 100,000 aboriginal children who were taken from their families by the government between about 1910 and 1970. The government believed the children would be better off in mainstream society than in aboriginal communities, which experts predicted would become extinct. Indigenous youth were placed in state homes or adopted by white foster parents. However, the relocations resulted in emotional trauma and widespread cultural devastation. Some indigenous Australians have even succeeded in winning reparations from the government to compensate them for the loss of identity they experienced. In 2008, Australian Prime Minister Kevin Rudd issued a formal apology to such individuals:

We reflect on [the Aborigines'] past mistreatment. We reflect in particular on the mistreatment of those who were stolen generations, this blemished chapter in our nation's history. . . . To the mothers and the fathers, the brothers and the sisters, for the breaking up of families and communities, we say sorry. And for the indignity and degradation thus inflicted on a proud people and a proud culture, we say sorry.[3]

they still encounter prejudice and discrimination. Some individuals view these indigenous peoples as no more than welfare recipients. They see Aborigines as natives who have not been able to keep up with the modernization that has shaped Australia since British colonization.

This prejudice negatively affects the continent's aboriginal culture. In regard to health issues and crime, those who have assimilated into mainstream society suffer disproportionately in comparison to other groups. Australian Aborigines also experience a higher unemployment rate and more limited educational opportunities.

Cultural Distinctions

There are usually cultural distinctions among a nation's various indigenous groups. For example, not all indigenous Australians are classified as aboriginal peoples. Torres Strait Islanders are an example of a local indigenous society that considers itself distinct from the continent's Aborigines. These people are native to islands off the coast of northern Queensland, Australia, near Papua New Guinea. Approximately 6 percent of indigenous Australians are listed as Torres Strait Islanders.

Asia's Adivasis

The continent of Asia is home to the world's largest indigenous populations. Of the estimated 370 million indigenous peoples on the planet, approximately 200 million live in the Asia region. Estimates for the number of Adivasis living in India alone run from 85 to 95 million people. Studies revealed that approximately half of the Adivasis fell below the national poverty line, versus 30 percent of the general population.

Many Adivasis live apart from mainstream society. Members of this indigenous group have been granted various land rights by the government. They use little to no advanced technology to farm the country's remote forest regions. However, corrupt officials and loggers sometimes operate outside the law to intrude upon their territory. They attempt to take advantage of local natural resources. In turn, the Adivasis' communities and agricultural practices are threatened.

"It is a cruel joke that people who can produce some of India's most exquisite handicrafts, who can distinguish hundreds of species of plants and animals, who can survive off the forests, the lands and the streams sustainably with no need to go to the market to buy food, are labeled as 'unskilled.'"[4]

—*Human rights activist C. R. Bijoy, 2003*

Advocates for indigenous peoples' rights continue to highlight the importance of these native groups. Indigenous peoples have made notable contributions to world culture and add to human diversity. For example, Taiwanese Aborigines are of particular interest to modern linguists. These experts think that Taiwan is where Austronesian languages originated.

The audience applauds Australian Prime Minister Kevin Rudd after he formally apologized to Australia's "stolen generations."

Juan Evo Morales Ayma, the president of Bolivia, took part in an indigenous ritual in 2010.

INDIGENOUS PEOPLES
OF THE AMERICAS

Most US history books contain accounts of fifteenth-century Italian explorer Christopher Columbus meeting various indigenous peoples who occupied the present-day Caribbean islands. They also tell tales of the

Spanish conquistadores who traveled in roughly the same era. They conquered the Aztecs, Incas, and Maya of South and Central America. Yet the journeys are often more focused on the European voyagers than the stories of the indigenous groups they met.

Today's indigenous peoples of North, Central, and South America belong to cultures and societies that existed in those parts of the world before the arrival of Columbus in the late 1400s. Some historians believe indigenous groups may have thrived in South America as far back as 35,000 years ago. Before European arrival, population estimates for the North and South American continents range from 30 million to 100 million. The impact of European colonization was disastrous for these groups. Diseases such as smallpox, influenza, and measles wiped out large percentages of native populations. In other cases, the people died during warfare with the Europeans or after being enslaved by them.

Uncontacted Peoples

Experts estimate that about 50 indigenous groups residing in the Amazon rain forest can be described as uncontacted peoples. They do not regularly communicate with or have any sort of dealings with outsiders. Little is known about these tribes. They continue to migrate deeper into the forest as mainstream groups move closer to their territories there.

Today, the status and social role of such cultures varies greatly from country to country. For example, indigenous peoples in Bolivia currently represent approximately 55 percent of the nation's total population. They fall into more than 30 groups. The largest of these indigenous cultures are the Quechua and the Aymara. Bolivia is the first South American country to allow its indigenous populations autonomy, or the right to self-government. On December 18, 2005, Juan Evo Morales Ayma was elected Bolivia's first indigenous president.

Peru also has a large indigenous population—almost 50 percent. The largest groups are the Quechua and the Aymara. Yet the country's indigenous cultures are at the center of many national controversies. In October 2006, human rights advocates referenced the fact that the government had not collected any recent statistical data about the nation's indigenous groups.

These groups often suffer from extreme poverty and lack of decent health care and educational benefits.

Indigenous Languages

Experts estimate that in the Americas, between 750 and 850 different indigenous languages are spoken by approximately 25.5 million people. The overwhelming majority of these individuals live in Central and South America. Only about 500,000 reside in North America. Linguists predict that, if greater efforts are not taken to preserve indigenous languages in North America, approximately 30 will remain in existence by 2050.

Peru's indigenous peoples must also fight to preserve their lands and their unrestricted access to natural resources. In addition, critics note that Peruvian government officials have allowed oil manufacturers to negatively affect rivers, vegetation, and wildlife that the natives rely upon for survival.

One human rights advocate summed up the plight of the nation's indigenous populations when he remarked, "In Peru, the poorest of the poor, the people who do not even have identity documents, the most neglected and abandoned, are indigenous people."[1] Similar problems exist for indigenous peoples in Central and North America too.

The Maya of Central America and Mexico

The Mayan people are among the most famous of the indigenous people in Central America and Mexico. Mayan people can trace their roots back 4,000 years. Today, they mainly live in Mexico, Belize, Guatemala, Honduras, and El Salvador. The ancient Maya are well known for advances they made in areas such as writing, astronomy, and the calendar system. In addition, sixteenth-century Spanish conquistadores marveled at their towering pyramid temples.

The arrival of Europeans in the Americas during the 1500s had a tremendous impact on Mayan culture. Large numbers were enslaved or died as a result of diseases brought with the Spanish. Today, many Maya have largely assimilated into mainstream society. Some work as farmers, laborers, or artisans. But overcrowding, unemployment, and local political unrest are among the challenges modern Maya face.

An Indigenous Nobel Peace Prize Winner

Rigoberta Menchú Tum, winner of the 1992 Nobel Peace Prize, is of Mayan descent. The same year she won the prize, she publicly summed up how she hoped the world would learn to perceive her people's culture. "We are not myths of the past, ruins in the jungle, or zoos," stated Menchú Tum. "We are people and we want to be respected, not to be victims of intolerance and racism."[2]

Advocates of indigenous cultures continue to crusade for increased rights for these individuals. They are eager to see Mayan languages more frequently used in the country's educational and legal systems. Some Maya find themselves at a disadvantage when they are tried in courtroom situations where the judge and attorneys speak only Spanish.

Many Maya object to government designation of their temples and sacred grounds as tourist attractions. They are also dissatisfied with their limited access to decent farmland. In Guatemala, for example, less

Hundreds of indigenous people gather near Mayan ruins in Mexico to explore solutions to environmental problems.

than 1 percent of agricultural producers who export goods to other nations have control over property that features the best soil and climate for farming. Instead, government officials and mining companies have been known to use these lands in manners in keeping with their best interests, not those of the indigenous groups.

As a result, some Maya find it nearly impossible to own successful farms. They, therefore, turn to seasonal or migratory labor as an alternate source of income. However, such positions often involve low wages and few workers' rights. Ultimately, the Maya are an example of the millions of indigenous Latin Americans struggling to overcome a wide array of social and political challenges.

New Lives in the United States

Some Maya move to the United States to escape political unrest or limited economic opportunities in their native countries. Unfortunately, many are forced to take low-paying jobs as migrant laborers on US farms. In their new homes, they often have few rights and are treated poorly by their employers. Xun Teratol, a Mayan advocate for indigenous peoples, described talking with such workers when he visited Immokalee, Florida. "Many were poor Maya who either had no work or were paid starvation wages in their own countries. They told us of their suffering, which was almost as bad as the abuses they have experienced here."[3]

Indigenous Cultures in the United States and Canada

Herbert Hale, who resides on the Cheyenne River Reservation in Cherry Creek, South Dakota, can attest to similar difficulties. He is one of approximately 3 million Native Americans who make up 563 tribes recognized in the United States. Members of these tribes are also referred to as American Indians. Farther north, approximately 1 million First Nations people claim indigenous origins in Canada. Separate indigenous populations that are part of the Inuit, Métis, and Hawaiian cultures exist throughout the continent as well.

As Hale's story proves, individuals with these backgrounds must often cope with poverty and social inequality. This was not always the case. But life began to change for indigenous peoples when British, French, Spanish, and Portuguese settlers began arriving in North America during the sixteenth and seventeenth centuries. These European explorers were eager to claim the continent's rich forests and fertile valleys and plains.

Their ambitions led to conflicts with North America's indigenous populations. Sometimes white settlers clashed with

A Tragic Journey for Indigenous Americans

Native Americans and early US citizens share a history that is not always filled with happy memories. Among the most painful of these is the Trail of Tears. Approximately 15,000 Cherokee Native Americans were forced to march to territory west of the Mississippi River during the late 1830s. Though much of the tribe initially resided in Georgia, both white settlers and several US officials were eager to claim local Native American lands that were rich in gold and ripe for development. As a result, politicians such as President Andrew Jackson fought for legislation that would allow the government to remove indigenous peoples from their homes and relocate them farther west. The Trail of Tears is so named because approximately 4,000 Cherokee died from starvation and sickness along the journey they endured between Georgia and what is now the state of Oklahoma.

"I saw the helpless Cherokees arrested and dragged from their homes, and driven at the bayonet point into the stockades," recalled one soldier who had been ordered to escort the Native Americans across the Mississippi. "The trail of the exiles was a trail of death."[4]

local native groups in episodes of actual warfare. On other occasions, indigenous peoples were moved to reservations. Many perished from diseases introduced by Europeans.

Today, Canadian and US citizens are working toward greater appreciation and understanding of indigenous cultures. But this does not mean that discrimination and inequality no longer exist. Like so many indigenous populations in other parts of the world, those in North America face dilemmas ranging from social prejudice to economic disadvantage. For example, in 2004, more than 24 percent of Native Americans lived below the poverty line.

According to government employees working for Indian and Northern Affairs Canada (INAC), similar issues impact its country's indigenous cultures. "The quality of life for Aboriginal people is lower than the general average for Canada," INAC reported in December 2008. "Life expectancy is shorter, job possibilities are narrower, and the rates for suicide, alcoholism and drug abuse are higher."[5] These realities are often the result of many factors, including indigenous peoples' ongoing struggles to win a meaningful political voice.

Rigoberta Menchú Tum has worked to fight for the rights of women and of the Mayan people.

Members of Bolivia's indigenous population march through the streets of La Paz in 2008. Indigenous groups often have their own laws and leaders.

PERSPECTIVES ON POLITICAL INDEPENDENCE

One of the criteria used to identify indigenous peoples is whether they existed before a particular nation was colonized or taken over by a foreign power. Before the Spanish invaded South America or the British set foot in

Australia, the native populations in those places already had their own political systems in place. Several indigenous groups around the globe have blended into modern mainstream cultures that are led by a president, king, or some other sort of leader or government body. These indigenous individuals are often guided in their decision making by national laws. They also try to participate in voting processes and educational, economic, and health-care programs sponsored by state agencies.

Regardless, assimilated indigenous groups frequently find they lack a significant political voice. This makes it difficult for them to enjoy all the rights and privileges usually associated with citizenship. In addition, indigenous peoples sometimes discover that supporting a nation's official political system is not always the best way to preserve their cultures.

It is common for these people to become frustrated when they try to demonstrate to lawmakers and politicians why the government needs to play a larger part in protecting their heritage. As a result, indigenous peoples often find themselves disappointed. Some feel that officials treat them like uneducated children, not bothering to consult them on issues ranging from land rights to the use of natural resources.

Because of this treatment, some groups seek increased autonomy, which is also referred to as self-determination or self-government. In general, indigenous peoples are eager to have more control over their own lands and resources. They want to determine social and economic issues based on a political structure of *their* choosing.

At the same time, they realize international issues will continue to impact their lives. Trade agreements and human rights controversies are relevant topics that many indigenous groups want to be able to discuss with local leaders and larger organizations such as the UN. Depending on the group, indigenous peoples may seek varying levels of autonomy and may not desire a complete break with a country's government. Rather, they would like increased authority over areas that affect them specifically. These include issues such as land distribution and public education.

Choosing Words Carefully

Sometimes a few simple words can make a huge difference in political debates surrounding indigenous autonomy. For example, those individuals who support indigenous peoples' rights to self-government in Bolivia talk about establishing a *pluri-national country*. Opponents of indigenous autonomy refer to their preference for an *intercultural state*. The first term implies a nation made up of several self-governing territories. The second describes a country that is home to and respectful of various cultures.

The Advantages of Autonomy

Bolivia made news headlines for becoming the first South American country to officially declare that its indigenous peoples had the right to self-government. A new national constitution adopted in early 2009 refers to Bolivia as being pluri-national, or made up of multiple nations. It provides for measures that allowed the country's 36 indigenous groups to vote for greater autonomy in December of that year.

Thanks to this legislation, indigenous peoples living in designated territories can draft their own laws and raise taxes. They are now able to make independent decisions regarding economic development and the use of natural resources. Advocates of autonomy believe that these new rights will help indigenous peoples maintain cultural elements that might otherwise be lost or overshadowed by more mainstream groups.

A Time of Autonomy Movements

The indigenous inhabitants of Mexico and Central and South America are gaining global recognition for their twenty-first-century efforts toward achieving autonomy. "Latin America is living [in] a time of autonomy movements," commented attorney and social analyst Francisco López Bárcenas in 2008. "[W]e must celebrate that many indigenous . . . communities . . . have enlisted in the construction of autonomous governments, unleashing processes where they test new forms of understanding rights [and] imagine other ways to exercise power. . . . It is certain that there is no going back to the past."[1]

A Subject Sparking Violent Debate

Different opinions on the subject of indigenous autonomy have sparked bloody protests in several South and Central American countries. In Bogotá, Colombia, the army and police clashed with indigenous protestors in fall 2008. The event resulted in violence that included the use of live ammunition, armored vehicles, and helicopters. One spokesperson for local indigenous groups later recalled the intensity of the unrest. "It was terrible, and so unfair," he reported. "We had no weapons. We only have our ceremonial staffs which [symbolize] authority."[4]

Miguel IPAM, the coordinator of the Indigenous Land Management that is part of the Confederation of Indigenous Peoples of Bolivia in the eastern portion of the country, predicted that self-government would even help preserve indigenous languages. "We are developing new curricula for our schools," he explained in 2009. "First, children will learn who we are and will learn our languages. After that [this knowledge] will go into the region, country and the rest of the world."[2]

Indigenous peoples across the globe have voiced similar confidence in the advantages of autonomy. "Initiatives developed on the ground, by the people for the people, have a far greater likelihood of working," emphasized Linda Burney, an aboriginal Australian social services employee.[3] In the past, that nation's government has historically passed laws and made decisions based on

In the United States, Native American tribes have certain guaranteed rights and freedoms, but they are still subject to the US federal government.

what mainstream officials consider best for various aboriginal cultures. However, such politicians often have limited input from indigenous peoples.

Opposing Attitudes and Additional Concerns

Not everyone shares this optimism about granting political autonomy to indigenous peoples. Some individuals argue that creating countries that consist of several independent nations sets the scene for chaos. They worry that autonomy increases tensions between indigenous cultures and mainstream society by further separating these two groups along ethnic or racial lines.

Some opponents of indigenous autonomy are worried about their own interests. In Bolivia, for instance, wealthier citizens and national officials understand all that the self-government of native cultures would entail. Indigenous peoples would win greater rights to some of the country's best farmlands, as well as those that are rich in natural resources. Certain Bolivian politicians and members of the

Native American Autonomy

The US government views various tribal groups as domestic dependent nations. This essentially means that they have more sovereignty, or independent authority, than states and local municipalities. Native Americans are permitted limited autonomy, but they are still subject to regulation by the US federal government. Controversies frequently arise over land and economic issues that pit tribal regulations against those of state agencies.

nation's upper class are concerned about losing their claims to these areas and the tax revenue they collect on them.

Another argument against autonomy questions if indigenous peoples are prepared to govern themselves. Are they able to control the majority of their economic activity? As IPAM admitted, some newly independent groups in Bolivia consist of no more than 1,000 individuals. He noted that autonomy would probably be more effective in the

Prepared for Empowerment?

Some opponents of indigenous autonomy have expressed concern about limited training in professional management among these indigenous groups. These critics argue that, to independently survive in the modern world, indigenous peoples need to be able to make effective economic and political decisions. Yet, while many indigenous groups welcome training that would better prepare them for the challenges of self-government, others are resistant to it.

It is no wonder that indigenous groups feel condescended to when the idea of teaching them how to run their own societies comes up. In most cases, their civilizations date back tens of thousands of years. This issue also stirs resentment among certain groups who point out that their lack of professional education and training is due to prejudice that has shut them out of mainstream political systems.

Finally, many are hesitant about further blending into other cultures by adopting the practices involved in mainstream politics and community management. Though opponents of indigenous autonomy insist that those groups do not possess the skills necessary for self-government, several of these individuals assert that they are capable of running their own communities using their own traditions and values.

context of larger communities. Yet joining together various indigenous groups to increase the population of a particular self-governed area presents its own set of complications. It means coordinating cultures with different dialects, traditions, and overall ways of life.

"We need to improve the organizational structure and make it clear how decisions are made and who is responsible in each instance," IPAM remarked in 2009 while discussing the concept of indigenous autonomy in Bolivia.[5] Yet whether indigenous peoples across the globe have complete, partial, or no political independence, they still face a number of obstacles. One of the largest is finding new and successful ways to preserve their cultures within a modern world that sometimes refuses to accept or understand them. ⌐

Mexican women attend the Continental Indigenous Encounter. This annual meeting unites indigenous groups from North, Central, and South America.

Ian Khama, president of Botswana, has expressed his opinion that the Bushmen's ways of life are out of date.

STRUGGLING FOR
CULTURAL SURVIVAL

Between 1997 and 2005, government officials in Botswana forced thousands of African Bushmen off their ancestral lands in the Central Kalahari Game Reserve (CKGR). In the 1980s, diamonds were discovered in the lands occupied by the Bushmen, making the land extremely valuable. At the time of the removals, local politicians claimed they were sending their nation's indigenous peoples to resettlement camps so they could further develop their culture and preserve certain natural areas. Yet many advocates of indigenous rights—and at least one government official—said that African lawmakers were truly motivated by greed. The government even cut off the Bushmen's access to water.

The heated controversy that exploded over the Bushmen's forced migration made news headlines around the world. Yet it was perhaps a minister of local government named Margaret Nasha who sparked the most immediate and intense outrage. She described the events at the CKGR as being similar to moving animals. "Sometimes I equate it to the elephants," she remarked. "We once had the same problem when we wanted to cull the elephants and people said 'no.'"[1] These comments infuriated some.

These various attempts by the government to explain its ill treatment of the Bushmen did have one positive outcome. Its actions made society more aware of how destructive discrimination against indigenous peoples is—as well as how real and powerful it remains in the twenty-first century.

DIFFERENT FORMS OF DISCRIMINATION

Discrimination against indigenous groups can take many forms. In certain instances, it is strikingly obvious. In Chile, for example, indigenous people known as the Mapuche routinely clash with local police in their fight to reclaim ancestral lands. In October 2009, however, the conflict took on a disturbing new dimension. Various Mapuche reported that Chilean police had—for no obvious reason—begun attacking their children with pellets and tear gas. Indigenous activists protested such assaults and called on human rights groups to help them put an end to the attacks.

Similar violence against indigenous peoples has erupted in

Horses gave Mapuche warriors in Chile an advantage when fighting to protect their land.

other parts of the world too, including Victoria, Australia. One resident of that state explained how prejudice was at the root of a wave of brutality against Aborigines living there. "At the moment," she observed, "we have a group of non-Aboriginal youth getting around calling themselves the KAC (Kill All Coons)."[4] *Coon* is an insulting name for members of Australia's aboriginal population. This term and others like it are sometimes found scrawled on buildings and in public common areas frequently

Advocates of Australia's indigenous peoples have recently condemned that nation's government for repealing various anti-racial discrimination laws that had previously protected aboriginal populations. Officials claim they suspended this legislation so they could address mounting reports of child sex abuse in certain indigenous communities.

As a result, however, legislators have instituted a series of controversial restrictions that only apply to Aborigines. These include bans on alcohol and rules regarding how welfare checks can be spent. Human rights advocates note that these measures are discriminatory because they do not affect any of Australia's other racial groups. Indigenous Affairs Minister Jenny Macklin observed in 2009 that changes to legislation had "left Aboriginal people feeling hurt, betrayed and less worthy than other Australians."[5]

used by that nation's indigenous peoples. As with violence, racists often use vandalism to demonstrate their discrimination against these groups.

Yet prejudice against indigenous cultures is not always this overt. Discrimination commonly takes the form of social misunderstanding or disapproval and the idea that indigenous groups are primitive or animalistic. People may not display these attitudes through obviously aggressive behavior. However, their misconceptions have a negative impact on members of the world's earliest civilizations.

Urged to Assimilate

Some people blame the disadvantages faced by indigenous groups on their lack of assimilation to the world that has developed around them. They believe that indigenous peoples would be better off blending into mainstream society. This view is not necessarily rooted in cultural hatred. More often, it stems from a lack of appreciation for the unique backgrounds that these groups represent.

People who encourage indigenous cultures to assimilate usually believe they are helping them adapt to a modern world. They think the poverty that regularly affects indigenous groups would not be so powerful if their members learned how to blend in with the economic and social mainstream.

This approach relies upon the idea that indigenous

Instructed to Abandon Indigenous Identity

Native American boarding schools were not intended to help Native Americans blend into mainstream society while simultaneously preserving their own cultural traditions. Instead, instructors at these institutions often believed that it was necessary to "kill the Indian and save the man."[6] School officials also thought that strict and sometimes harsh discipline was justified if it would help Native Americans become "completely 'civilized.'"[7]

For many students, however, attending boarding school was not completely negative. Several Native Americans later recalled how standards of living were far higher there than on reservations. Yet they also acknowledged that such benefits came at a high price. They lost their abilities to think as individuals and as members of a unique culture.

"On the reservations there was no electricity or running water," one former student explained. "When kids came to the boarding school they had these things—showers and clean clothes—and they ate decent food. . . . My main criticism of the boarding school is that . . . your whole life was governed. As a result, you didn't learn how to become an independent thinker."[8]

peoples are somehow inferior and need to forsake their old ways of life to learn how to act and survive in modern times. This is especially ironic, given that many indigenous groups have managed to preserve their cultures for thousands of years.

Even so, the indigenous groups often find themselves struggling in the process, especially when society is continually urging them to learn new ways. The stories of various Native American tribes are evidence of this fact. The nineteenth and early twentieth centuries were particularly challenging periods for these groups. They were often at odds with white settlers and US government officials who were anxious to expand America's borders by claiming tribal lands.

People from Christian missionaries to politicians have been known to pressure Native Americans into blending in with

A Threat to Mental and Emotional Health

Stereotypes and prejudice have serious long-term consequences that often affect the mental and emotional health of indigenous peoples. A 2004 report released by the United Nations Children's Fund (UNICEF) indicated that discrimination frequently leads to crises of self-esteem and identity among these populations. In turn, indigenous communities tend to suffer from higher rates of alcoholism, substance abuse, depression, and suicide.

white culture. Whites urged them to dress in traditional Western clothes and abandon lifestyles that focused on hunting and gathering to instead work on farms. In addition, countless tribes were encouraged to give up their languages and learn to speak English.

Native Americans who chose not to assimilate were faced with limited alternatives. They could either leave their homes and move to reservations far west of the Mississippi River, or they could expect harassment and social rejection from the whites who were encroaching upon their territories. Some tribes were not even given the freedom to decide between these options. In many cases, the US government forcibly moved them to reservations.

Even those indigenous peoples who were permitted to remain on their lands and did their best to blend into white culture still regularly

History of Fishing Rights in the Pacific Northwest

In the Pacific Northwest, fish has been a staple in the diets of Native Americans. As the nation's borders expanded, native groups in these areas entered into treaties with the US government. The settlers in these areas were primarily interested in mining and farming, but the native tribes were interested in keeping their access to the rivers that provided them with fish, especially salmon.

However, the treaties honoring the natives' right to fish began to be violated. In 1913, some natives were even arrested for fishing on their own land. As commercial fishing increased, the amount of available fish decreased, further hurting the natives. In the 1960s and 1970s, natives engaged in "fish-ins," where they protested regulations by engaging in illegal fishing activities. Numerous legal battles have ensued, and the controversy endures today.

experienced discrimination. Native American children were frequently taken away from their families and placed in special boarding schools. These schools were especially popular from the 1880s to the 1920s. Instructors at these institutions taught tribal youth how to dress, speak, and act more like white US citizens.

Nearly 100 years later, the majority of people living in the United States have adopted more progressive attitudes toward local tribes. Yet the pressure to blend in has not disappeared. A study conducted in 2006 revealed that several Native American children are hesitant to learn tribal languages because they want to appear "less Indian."[9] Like so many indigenous peoples, they are torn between mixing into mainstream society and accepting their cultural heritage.

In Montana, Pauline Standing Rock teaches students the Cree language.
Many native languages are in danger of dying out.

Adivasis in India who are too poor to pay for a wedding participate in mass marriage ceremonies.

PLAGUED BY POVERTY

If cultural differences sometimes lay at the root of the discrimination faced by indigenous peoples, so do economic distinctions. "Poverty casts its darkest shadows upon indigenous people," Boutros Boutros-Ghali, UN secretary-general from 1992 to 1996, observed in a speech delivered on August 9, 1995.[1] This was the first International Day of the World's Indigenous People. Precise statistics vary, but there is little doubt as to the accuracy of his statement.

In Guatemala, for example, 87 percent of the indigenous population lives below the poverty line. More than 50 percent of Botswana's Bushmen are also reported to be at that economic level. But developing nations are not the only areas where hardship defines day-to-day life for indigenous groups. In 2006, a study in Canada revealed that its indigenous peoples were twice as likely to be unemployed as nonindigenous citizens.

Numerous factors lead to these economic challenges. These include loss of land and lack of support from mainstream government systems. Additionally, the destruction or overuse of natural resources can hurt indigenous peoples. Discrimination in the workplace frequently impacts the rights of indigenous peoples.

The economy influences many aspects of people's lives, regardless of whether they claim indigenous backgrounds. For indigenous groups, however, problems such as poverty and unemployment require careful examination because they are also connected to issues of cultural survival. Indigenous peoples struggle to maintain economic independence in a world filled with societies that rely heavily upon fast-paced industry and highly developed technology.

Many indigenous peoples want to preserve their heritage by using traditional agricultural and manufacturing practices that reflect their respect for the environment. Others have waged long and unsuccessful battles for the right to hunt and live on their ancestral lands.

Bereft of the Buffalo

For centuries, Native Americans have relied on the resources available in their tribal lands. For example, Native Americans living on the Great Plains relied heavily upon the American bison, or buffalo. Though they hunted the animal, they also had a deep respect for it. The animal provided food, clothing, and a variety of other everyday items.

During the late nineteenth century, white hunters shot and killed millions of these creatures, driving them to the brink of extinction. Much of this slaughter was done for sport or to clear the path for railroads. It also was instrumental in driving an increasing number of Native Americans onto reservations. They were faced with the prospect of starving if they remained on their own lands.

US officials hoped that eliminating the buffalo would compel tribes to abandon their hunter-gatherer lifestyles for more settled existences as farmers. In addition, they were eager to push Native Americans onto reservations so they could claim new territories and expand US borders. By killing off the buffalo, these individuals did an enormous amount of damage to indigenous cultures and their abilities to independently survive.

Yet members of mainstream society do not always support such efforts or appreciate their significance. Not all nonindigenous peoples fully grasp that, if economic hardship continues to plague their indigenous counterparts, several unique cultures will inevitably face extinction.

The Example of the Adivasis

It would be impossible to list all the individual factors that contribute to the poverty affecting indigenous groups across the globe. This is due to a variety of cultural, geographic, and political distinctions. For instance, Botswana's Bushmen suffer because they are routinely denied access to their ancestral hunting grounds. Lakota Native Americans living on reservations in South Dakota are confronted with a lack of local employment opportunities.

Nonetheless, experts generally point to a series of problems that

Adivasi Ideals

The Adivasis are willing to work hard to escape poverty, establish a greater sense of self-reliance, and preserve their identity as indigenous people. Dr. Ganesh Devy is an activist and writer who has worked extensively with India's various native tribes. In 2007, he summed up how the Adivasis perceive the path to economic growth. He wrote, "Without self-reliance, without standing on our own feet it is meaningless to even talk about development. . . . Everything is possible but we will have to work hard for it. Nature is more important than humans. The society is more important than a person."[2]

repeatedly play a major role in furthering economic disadvantage within indigenous communities. Abuse of these peoples' rights to land and natural resources is a particularly destructive influence and occurs on practically every continent where they reside.

Deforestation, overhunting, and pollution threaten the traditional methods most indigenous civilizations rely upon to survive and prosper. Certain Adivasi tribes in India can attest to this fact. Many have been moved from their homes as the government allows mining and logging companies to take over their lands. In addition to watching their villages destroyed, the Adivasis are forced to abandon their farms, hunting grounds, and water sources. In Karnataka, a state in India, approximately 85 percent of the Adivasi population lives below the poverty line.

Fighting the government for adequate compensation or the means to rebuild communities and agricultural projects is typically fruitless. It is common for officials in India and other countries to side with large corporations that promise to boost the nation's economy with their development of the land.

Rather than starve, some Adivasis seek employment as migrant laborers in mines or on construction sites and plantations. While these jobs may serve as a means of income, they frequently involve poor working conditions. Since the Adivasis have limited government representation, they also have few sources of protection they can turn to if their labor rights are violated.

Many employers realize this and abuse their indigenous workers. They might withhold payment for services or offer laborers less than the required minimum wage. Others force employees to toil for long hours or fail to provide safe and sanitary workplace conditions. Child labor, sexual harassment, and physical abuse are also common problems that Adivasi migrant workers experience.

What limited income these indigenous laborers bring back to their families is overshadowed by the fact that their jobs often require them to leave home for weeks or even months at a time. In some cases,

A Drain on Educational Resources

Economic disadvantage impacts educational resources available to indigenous groups. Families who want to place their children in mainstream schools and colleges often find it difficult to pay for tuition, transportation, tutoring, and other related costs. Even those indigenous peoples who prefer their youth to be educated only within their specific communities are affected by poverty. Children frequently must work at extremely young ages to help support their families. In turn, this leaves little time for schooling or other forms of learning that might occur within the community.

Adivasis must also cope with the realities of working for mainstream companies whose philosophies run in contrast to their own cultural values. This is because indigenous peoples sometimes have distinctive beliefs and attitudes about nature and development.

For example, the majority of Adivasi tribes prefer to rely on hunting and agricultural practices that are respectful of the environment. They pay close attention to the naturally occurring cycles and seasons in the forests around them. They are cautious about killing animals or harvesting plants that appear to be scarce.

Though some mainstream corporations try to be conscious of how their actions impact ecology, they are also driven by advanced technology and industry that allow them to build, farm, and manufacture on a large scale. These companies focus on successfully turning profits. They are not always concerned with finding new ways to survive on the land while preserving cultural heritage.

These different ways of thinking can often lead to situations in which groups such as the Adivasis end up in jobs providing low pay, limited rights, and an absence of the traditions and values that shape their cultural identities. Unfortunately, because they are frequently deprived of the means to independently operate their own farms and businesses, the alternative is sometimes starvation. Yet these desperate economic circumstances are not unique to the Adivasis. Further complicating matters is the crushing poverty that results in limited access to health care for these indigenous groups. Lack of health care can bring about a decline in their overall physical and mental well-being.

Economic Impacts on Indigenous Health Care

Many of the challenges that indigenous groups face are part of a vicious cycle related to economic disadvantage. The poverty that impacts their communities often means limited health-care resources. In turn, it is difficult for people to

Improving Indigenous Health Care

Several medical and human rights experts agree that improving health care within indigenous communities cannot be accomplished through funding alone. They believe that it is also important to involve the people themselves in promoting better living conditions and higher standards of physical and mental wellness. This approach entails everything from providing training to indigenous health-care workers to helping such groups incorporate their cultural beliefs and practices into modern medical philosophies and treatments.

In Montana, Ada White holds a picture of her great niece Ta'Shon. Ta'Shon's cancer was misdiagnosed by the local Native American medical service, and the girl died soon after.

prosper when they are struggling with everything from diseases to depression.

Indigenous groups that rely on government agencies for health-care assistance frequently find they are underrepresented. Therefore, they do not receive much-needed funding. Certain communities located in remote regions do not have regular access to physicians, hospitals, or current medical information regarding disease transmission and treatment.

Those groups that do not rely on government-run health assistance often prefer to use their own traditional medicines and healing methods. Sometimes, these involve the use of specific plants, herbs, and religious ceremonies. Yet economic disadvantage affects these individuals as well. When indigenous peoples are evicted from their lands or forced to leave to find work, they have no choice but to reprioritize their time and resources. Homeless and thrown into migratory lifestyles, they may not have the opportunity to practice customary rituals and produce their own medicines when they are sick.

As politicians and developers move indigenous groups off their lands, they also reduce their ability to farm, hunt, and rely upon a steady source of food and freshwater. This can lead to poor nutrition. In addition, when the threat of starvation looms, people become desperate to survive. They may turn to crime or physically taxing jobs as migrant laborers and sweatshop workers.

It is not surprising that indigenous groups also report high rates of depression, substance abuse, and suicide. Experts believe these are directly linked to their experiences with poverty and discrimination. Diseases such as tuberculosis, hepatitis, malaria, and HIV have been known to spread rapidly throughout indigenous communities. These problems are especially acute in overcrowded areas. It is not uncommon for average life expectancy to be decreased in these areas as well.

According to a report issued by the UN, the quality of life for Australia's Aborigines ranks among the poorest on Earth. Researchers estimated that, on average, these individuals can expect to live about ten to 17 years less than nonindigenous peoples. In light of these bleak realities, human rights advocates, political officials, and average world citizens are continually trying to develop new ways to aid indigenous populations. ⁓

Statistics on Suicide

Research indicates that Aboriginal men living in Australia are three times more likely to commit suicide than members of that nation's nonindigenous male population. In North America, suicide is the second leading cause of death for Native Americans and Alaska natives aged 15 to 34. Suicide rates for these groups are approximately twice the national average.

Australia's aboriginal populations have struggled to maintain their unique cultural identities in a growing, fast-paced world.

*Fair trade aims to bring fair wages to producers in developing countries.
Fair trade products include coffee, bananas, and cocoa.*

SEARCHING FOR
SOLUTIONS THROUGH
FAIR TRADE

conomic stability and independence—or
the absence of those things—do a great
deal to shape many aspects of indigenous peoples'
lives. As a result, some experts believe an economic
solution might help.

Specifically, fair trade involves agricultural and business practices that are intended to benefit workers and producers in developing areas. It is rooted in several principles that all support this idea, and it is often regarded as both a social and economic movement. Advocates of fair trade emphasize that it is intended to help the world's disadvantaged groups achieve self-sufficiency and economic independence without sacrificing their traditions and cultural identities. This status is especially important to indigenous peoples but can be difficult for them to attain.

An Overview of the Approach

In most instances of fair trade, retail companies in developed nations agree to purchase goods from producers in less-established areas. Ideally, fair trade involves retailers paying competitive or above-market prices to producers in developing countries who demonstrate that they meet certain social, ethical, and environmental standards. For example, retail organizations that promote fair trade advertise that the farmers and manufactures they buy from guarantee their laborers livable wages and safe working conditions.

Several organizations also encourage respect for the environment by dealing only with producers who avoid the use of pesticides and other ecologically harmful substances. Those involved in fair trade also aim to raise social awareness. They hope that their economic decisions make the public more conscious of the problems that plague the world's disadvantaged groups, including indigenous peoples.

Retail corporations that support fair trade usually negotiate

At the Mercy of the Middleman

Advocates of fair trade argue that the poverty and lack of technology in indigenous communities put producers who have to deal with middlemen at a disadvantage. Whereas growers and manufacturers who are involved in fair trade sell directly to retailers, those who are not are frequently at the mercy of intermediary agencies. These middlemen are sometimes producers' primary links to mainstream society and international economics.

Haven Bourque, a spokesperson for Trans-Fair USA, observed:

If you're growing cocoa in Ghana and you're not part of a cooperative, you're probably illiterate. You don't have a truck, so you're dependent on the middleman to come to you. You don't have a scale, so you're dependent on his scale as well. And you certainly don't have a cell phone, so you don't know what the price of cocoa is today on the New York commodities exchange.[1]

Fair trade producers generally would have an advantage in such situations. There are no middlemen driving down prices as they prepare to buy from producers. In addition, farmers and manufacturers who belong to fair trade cooperatives communicate openly and regularly about topics such as pricing and the current international economic situation.

with and buy directly from producers themselves. These retailers promise to pay farmers and manufacturers enough to cover the cost of production, plus an additional premium. It is common for fair trade producers to belong to cooperatives. In these associations, members work together. Growers and manufacturers who participate in cooperatives retain their independence but share resources. They also market and sell their goods as a larger group. Members of fair trade cooperatives typically express interest in further developing the towns and villages in which they operate.

Because producers control their own businesses, they have the freedom to use their profits to sustain their communities and to make them more independent. Many fair trade agreements require them to do just that. Farm owners and manufacturers might decide to give back to their communities by funding local schools or health-care programs.

Fair Trade Handicrafts and Art

Though many consumers think of coffee, bananas, or chocolate when they envision products that are marketed as fair trade certified, cultural handicrafts and art are also items that often carry this label. From woven baskets to colorful tapestries, such goods frequently provide shoppers with added insight into the heritage of the indigenous groups who fashioned them. As one volunteer working with a nonprofit organization in Argentina explained, "Crafts are not the same as just any product that you buy in a store or supermarket. Handicrafts have a symbolic value that expresses years of culture, wisdom and ways of life of (indigenous) communities."[2]

Conducting fair trade according to these principles is supposed to encourage self-empowerment of groups who might otherwise be exploited or discriminated against by mainstream society. Perhaps they do not have access to free, fair markets. For indigenous peoples, fair trade ideally aids them in their fight to preserve their cultural heritage. Fair trade is designed to allow such individuals the authority to create, own, and operate businesses that are run according to their value systems and particular ways of life.

Impacts on International Economics

Fair trade items include bananas, flowers, sugar, tea, coffee, handicrafts, cocoa, wine, chocolates, and cotton. But how do average consumers know if they are purchasing a product that is the result of this market system?

The majority of foods and wares created through fair trade practices carry some sort of label or certification mark imprinted by one of several national and international federations. Fairtrade International (FLO), the World Fair Trade Organization (WFTO), and the Fair Trade Federation (FTF) are a few examples of these groups. Each is committed to promoting fair trade and monitoring how it is practiced throughout the world. Many consumers are drawn to buying items produced through this market approach because they feel they can use simple shopping habits to promote positive social, environmental, and economic change.

Consumers do not necessarily spend significantly more for fair trade goods just because retailers pay producers above-market prices. However, fair trade products do usually cost more than similar non-fair trade products. Some consumers have deemed the price difference worth paying to support the fair trade cause. "The difference is that the farmers are getting the fairest deal out of the export price possible," explained Charlotte Opal, author and new products manager at TransFair USA, which is based out of Oakland, California. "In the traditional supply chain, the middlemen and the exporters keep most of the profits, and the farmers are left with very little."[3]

By cutting out the middlemen, producers hope to receive a greater profit without consumers having to pay substantially higher costs. This fact—as well as the social and ethical benefits connected to fair trade—have made it an increasingly popular market system. Economic reports are evidence of its continued growth. The FTF reported that in 2008, people around the world spent approximately $4 billion on foods and wares that were certified as products of fair trade. This was a growth of 22 percent.

At the conclusion of 2009, researchers estimated that there were 827 fair trade–certified producer organizations representing more than 1.5 million farmers and laborers across the globe. It is believed that a substantial number of these people are members of indigenous groups. Yet the realities of fair trade and the actual benefits this market approach has on such individuals remain somewhat controversial.

Millions attended Live 8 concerts held in ten cities worldwide. The concerts aimed to increase aid to developing countries and promote fair trade.

Proponents of fair trade say the practice helps indigenous peoples create and sell handicrafts that have cultural value.

Mixed Views on Fair Trade

or some indigenous peoples, fair trade has proved an ideal solution to several of the social and economic troubles they face. Many Mayan cocoa farmers living in Belize have observed positive changes since joining local fair trade cooperatives.

From the perspective of Anastasia—a mother of seven children—this market approach has provided her family with independence and the means to receive an education. "[My] oldest is already in high school," she noted in 2009. "We hope that all the children will go to school because of the money we receive from growing [cocoa]. Currently we have 2 to 3 acres [.8 to 1.2 ha] and are planting more."[1]

Yet not everyone views fair trade in such a positive light. Some economic experts point out that Anastasia's story is not necessarily reflective of the majority of situations. These critics insist that fair trade truly aids only those individuals who have enough money to own small farms or businesses.

These critics also note that the people who suffer the greatest poverty and require the most economic support are migrant workers and sweatshop laborers. The men and women who fall into these categories—and who often claim indigenous backgrounds—are not in a position to own a small business. And they do not always have the opportunity to work at fair trade farms or cooperatives.

For this and other reasons, people who are against fair trade argue that it is only a front that plays on consumers' desires to be socially conscious.

"At best, fair trade is a marketing device that does the poor little good," remarked Tom Clougherty, policy director for the Adam Smith Institute in London, England, which researches and reports on issues related to economic policy. "At worst, it may inadvertently be harming some of the planet's most vulnerable people."[2] Clougherty's opinions and ideas, as well as those of people such as Anastasia, continue to shape the debate on how much fair trade truly benefits the world's indigenous populations.

Arguments Supporting Fair Trade

Advocates of fair trade are quick to respond to criticism by noting that this market approach has already improved the lives of millions of people in developing nations. They also emphasize that it is an effective way to preserve indigenous cultures. Supporters of fair trade believe that it allows these groups to maintain economic stability while simultaneously strengthening their communities.

They argue that indigenous peoples who participate in this market system are less likely to face long-term poverty. Advocates of fair trade insist that such individuals are not compelled to hunt for work in sweatshops or situations involving migratory labor. They do not have to leave their homes and communities to search for jobs that frequently offer limited rights and meager wages.

In addition, supporters of fair trade often discuss the fact that it benefits indigenous groups by promoting sustainable living. This describes a lifestyle that aims to conserve natural resources so future generations can take advantage of them. Farmers and manufacturers involved in fair trade generally limit their use of harmful chemicals, including various

Changing Children's Lives

People who support fair trade often point out how this market system improves the lives of indigenous children. On one level, producers frequently use a portion of their profits to further community development. This sometimes takes the form of scholarship funds or the construction of schools. The fact that fair trade encourages sustainable living is an additional benefit. Natural resources will be conserved so that younger generations will ultimately be able to use them.

From another angle, however, advocates of this market approach argue that it reduces incidents of child labor and exploitation within indigenous populations. Due to the poverty and lack of employment opportunities in indigenous communities, young people are sometimes forced to work in sweatshops or on plantations to earn extra income for their families. Others become trapped in situations involving drugs, prostitution, or human trafficking.

Those individuals who are in favor of fair trade note that certification standards strictly prohibit the use of child labor. They also insist that—thanks to the economic stability this market system intends to establish within indigenous communities—poverty is reduced and children are less pressured to sustain family income.

fertilizers and pesticides. Many rely on environmentally friendly methods of conserving soil. Several even plant trees as a way to provide necessary amounts of shade to certain crops.

This ecological awareness linked to fair trade protects indigenous cultures. It reinforces the environmental perspectives and values they hold. It ensures that groups already suffering from limited land rights are able to get the most use out of the areas in which they live for an extended period of time.

Advocates of fair trade feel that it preserves indigenous cultures in several other ways as well. They claim it raises social awareness about indigenous peoples and helps them to earn increased recognition in international economics. For instance, consumers in the United States who buy fair trade—certified coffee can often read on the package exactly who grew the beans and

Understanding Fair Trade

Many of the indigenous producers involved in fair trade have indicated that they wish they had a better understanding of the contracts, supply chain, and labeling system that shape their businesses. A percentage has also commented on how they want a greater voice in establishing the criteria for certification. Experts have suggested that indigenous producers might gain a better grasp on fair trade if they could visit retail locations where their items are sold. They also believe it would be beneficial for importers to periodically tour production sites. Some recommend that indigenous peoples be offered training in global marketing as well.

Fair trade products carry a special certification logo.

how the purchase is aiding that particular group. Supporters of this market system explain that it is also an opportunity for indigenous cultures to earn income by producing items that reflect their traditions and heritage. Textiles, jewelry, pottery, and art are just a few examples of the wares that bear fair trade—certified labels.

Regardless of the specific product being produced, advocates of this market approach note that one of its chief benefits is encouraging indigenous producers to give back to their communities. Producers frequently contribute a portion of their profits to development projects such as vaccination programs, scholarship funds, and the construction of schools, housing, and wells. These efforts undeniably support the growth and survival of indigenous cultures. However, people who are opposed to fair trade are quick to point out that they are not the only factors at play.

Alternate Views on Fair Trade

Critics of fair trade do not contest the idea that improving resources in developing communities is a positive thing. Nor do they feel that fair trade is the best way to accomplish this goal. Opposition to this market approach often focuses on the idea that the introduction of new industry and technology to such areas is a preferable method of achieving stability and growth.

Opponents of fair trade argue that it relies too heavily on consumers who essentially believe they are making a charitable contribution to indigenous cultures and other developing nations. If the cost for fair trade products is higher than a comparable product without the fair trade label, what happens if consumers are unable or not willing

to continue paying a higher price?
The farmers and manufacturers
are little better than "prisoners to
[the] market."[3] Opponents also
suggest that fair trade farmers and
manufacturers are granted a special
place in international economics.
The higher prices they receive for
their goods might be creating a false
economy that cannot be sustained.
Additionally, if a retailer decides
to stop selling fair trade items or
consumers lose interest, their profits
can be seriously impacted.

Minimal Benefits

Among those who
question the true ben-
efits of fair trade is Steve
Daley, who works with
an education-develop-
ment charity known as
WORLDwrite. The group
is based out of Lon-
don. "How can a few
extra pennies a day from
Fairtrade be celebrated as
an outstanding achieve-
ment for the poor?"
questioned Daley.[4]

Critics of this market approach also note that it
does not succeed in improving life for indigenous
peoples to the degree that average consumers believe
it does. Additionally, many wonder if fair trade
certification groups can accurately monitor their
producers to ensure that all standards are being
met. In 2006, an article by Hal Weitzman appeared
in the *Financial Times*, revealing that workers on a fair
trade farm in Peru were earning less than minimum
wage. The Fairtrade Foundation issued a response,
emphasizing the strength of their audit process

and declaring intent to investigate the claim. Opponents of fair trade emphasize that, with reality falling short of the ideal, there is scarce hope that the practice will provide long-term economic stability and growth to indigenous groups.

In addition, some critics suspect that it actually has the potential to worsen their situations. Not every indigenous person has the means to start his or her own farm or business, even with financial assistance from retailers who support fair trade. Those who do are sometimes unable to pay the fees associated with certification, which can range from $2,500 to $10,000 a year. Others simply do not choose to participate in fair trade based on their individual needs, opinions, and priorities. Unfortunately, it is frequently harder for smaller producers to compete with organizations that are guaranteed a role in the international

Confusing Consumers?

One common criticism of fair trade is that what consumers see is not necessarily what they get. For example, some experts argue that, while big-name companies such as Starbucks and Procter & Gamble claim to support fair trade, they only import and sell a limited amount of certified products. Certification labels do not distinguish between retailers who purchase 100 percent of their goods through fair trade and those who only buy 1 percent of their stock in this manner. This could potentially lead consumers to patronize certain businesses because they believe them to be more socially conscious than they actually are.

economy under the umbrella of fair trade. Some individuals believe that the higher prices retailers are willing to pay farmers and manufacturers worsen conditions for indigenous peoples who are not involved with this marketing approach. Some have proposed a different solution.

Fair Trade and Free Trade

Opponents of fair trade often believe that free trade is a better alternative for indigenous peoples and other disadvantaged groups living in developing nations. This market approach operates on the philosophy that the international economy should remain free of any unnecessary restrictions and management.

People who prefer free trade frequently feel that paying fair trade producers higher prices serves as a form of harmful interference and discourages healthy competition. They argue that offering special protection to the poor actually prevents them from fully participating in the international economy. These individuals insist that fair trade keeps indigenous cultures from learning how to seize opportunities that naturally arise in the world market.

Opponents of fair trade insist that it does more to make consumers feel good about themselves than it offers indigenous groups opportunities to preserve their identities, lands, and ways of life. Regardless of whether their opinions are correct, most individuals agree that there are other methods of protecting these cultures. They realize it is crucial to consider a wide range of solutions to help indigenous peoples survive in a twenty-first century world.

Critics of fair trade believe it creates false economies that cannot be sustained.

In India, an Adivasi beats a drum alongside Nitish Kumar, left, a public official.

OTHER EFFORTS TO PRESERVE INDIGENOUS CULTURES

As indigenous peoples struggle to preserve their cultures against the backdrop of modern society, many people are working to find the most effective methods of aiding them. On an international level, human rights groups such as the UN, the WB, and the ILO have launched campaigns to raise awareness about some of the issues these people face.

These organizations also attempt to help indigenous peoples achieve greater stability by contributing to community development projects that range from digging wells to vaccinating children. In addition, these groups and others like them publicly champion the rights of indigenous societies. Activists use the media and lobbying activities within national governments to draw attention to the abuses that they suffer.

In keeping with these efforts, the UN General Assembly adopted the United Nations Declaration on the Rights of Indigenous Peoples on September 13, 2007. This document consists of 46 articles that describe various privileges indigenous groups should under no circumstances be denied. These include self-determination, use and control of their lands, and freedom from discrimination. Technically, the declaration is not legally binding for the many nations that make up the UN. This means that member states would not face legal punishment if they violated the rights that are listed in the declaration.

Nevertheless, UN officials regard the document as representing a carefully constructed moral code that they urge people all over the world to apply to their daily lives. The declaration states the following truths in regard to indigenous populations:

Indigenous peoples are equal to all other peoples, while recognizing the right of all peoples to be different, to consider themselves different, and to be respected as such. . . . All peoples contribute to the diversity and richness of civilizations and cultures, which constitute the common heritage of humankind.[1]

Free and Equal

The United Nations Declaration on the Rights of Indigenous Peoples addresses topics ranging from autonomy to environmental conservation. Prior to the 46 articles that are listed in the document, its authors acknowledged that "the situation of indigenous peoples varies from region to region . . . and that the significance of national and regional particularities and various historical and cultural backgrounds should be taken into consideration."[2] They also stated that the declaration should be used "as a standard of achievement to be pursued in a spirit of partnership and mutual respect."[3] The articles that follow include discussion of some of the following rights:

Indigenous peoples and individuals are free and equal to all other peoples and individuals and have the right to be free from any kind of discrimination. . . . Indigenous peoples have the right to maintain and strengthen their distinct political, legal, economic, social and cultural institutions, while retaining their right to participate fully, if they so choose, in the political, economic, social and cultural life of the State.[4]

Despite the UN having asserted these guiding principles, it is still up to national and local governments to see that they enact legislation guided by these UN principles.

The Importance of Government and Political Support

Several human rights organizations have worked tirelessly to help indigenous groups preserve their cultural identities. Yet it is important that such efforts are reinforced by legal and political support. For instance, some nations draft legislation that is designed to shield indigenous peoples from discrimination. Thanks to these laws, individuals who believe they have been treated unfairly in settings ranging from country clubs to places of employment can file complaints. Depending on how a nation's legal system is structured, judges or other public officials can then determine if

Making Politicians More Culturally Aware

Indigenous peoples have frequently expressed the desire to see a greater number of mainstream politicians educate themselves about their unique cultural beliefs and traditions. Many groups currently feel that such officials automatically assume that they know what is best for indigenous persons when it comes to everything from government funding to land usage. "Life is getting harder for our people," a member of one Australian aboriginal community recently observed. "We are still being stigmatised, demoralised and disempowered. . . . The government needs to work with our people and not dictate to us."[5]

An Arizona student visits the Heard Museum, where an exhibit features information about Native American boarding schools.

an indigenous person has been discriminated against and how he or she should be compensated.

In other situations, governments can demonstrate their support for indigenous groups by respecting their claims to autonomy and protecting their rights to live on and use their land. Legislation is one way to do this, but it must be clearly explained and consistently enforced.

For example, in December 2006, judges in Botswana ruled that local Bushmen had been illegally evicted from the CKGR. These indigenous peoples went on to wage legal battles to access natural resources found there. A later ruling denied them the right to access water on that land. These circumstances have led several Bushmen to feel that the 2006 ruling is confusing and somewhat meaningless. One chief discussed the mixed emotions he experienced upon being allowed to move back to the reserve. He explained,

> We are back where we belong. . . . but life is very difficult and we are still scared that the court ruling is not a permanent thing—one of my brothers was stopped from coming back.[6]

Even with enhanced government support, laws that have been created to preserve indigenous cultures are likely not enough to guarantee that

The Power of the Media

Like politicians and members of human rights organizations, media workers also have the power to aid indigenous peoples. By covering stories about issues that impact these populations, writers and reporters keep the public's attention focused on important political, social, and economic topics. Some experts argue that in addition to mainstream newspapers, magazines, Web sites, and radio and television programming, media outlets organized and run by indigenous groups are an effective way to promote cultural preservation. These individuals believe that increased communication between indigenous peoples provides added opportunities for them to share their experiences and encourage community development.

these groups survive. Some volunteer groups have stepped in to help create an attitude of respect toward indigenous peoples.

Institutions That Support Indigenous Cultures

Various research centers, museums, and galleries across the globe concentrate their efforts on studying, celebrating, and preserving indigenous cultures. Many contain artwork or artifacts that reflect these groups' histories and traditions. A few examples include the Museum of Mayan Culture in Chetumal, Mexico, and the Australian Institute of Aboriginal and Torres Strait Islander Studies in Canberra, Australia. Such institutions generally aim to raise public awareness about the unique identities of indigenous peoples and their struggles in modern society.

The Impact of Everyday Efforts

In 2008, grade-schoolers at St. Monica School in Whitefish Bay, Wisconsin, sponsored clothing and school-supply drives to aid disadvantaged Lakota Native Americans. In 2009, a young Lakota woman named Autumn Two Bulls added entries to her blog about life on the Pine Ridge Reservation in South Dakota. Her goal in starting the online journal was to raise awareness of the issues on the reservation, including poverty and suicide.

These situations demonstrate how average citizens can take action in their daily lives to help protect and raise awareness of indigenous peoples. Though these instances

*An indigenous forum in Peru in 2008 drew Andean women.
Attendees discussed globalization and other issues.*

focus specifically on Lakota Native Americans in the
United States, similar efforts can be used to assist
groups ranging from the Adivasis of India to the
Aborigines of Australia.

Educational campaigns, community fund-
raisers, and programming created to encourage
appreciation of cultural diversity are just a few
examples. In addition, it is often beneficial for
individuals with indigenous backgrounds and
those of more mainstream groups to collaborate

their efforts. Promoting open communication and cultural acceptance goes a long way toward ending discrimination and the conflicts and dilemmas that accompany it.

It is up to average citizens, as well as government officials and international human rights organizations, to ensure that cultures that have existed for tens of thousands of years do not disappear during the twenty-first century. From the Bushmen to the Maya to the Lakota, indigenous peoples across the globe have made countless contributions to civilization. Their traditions, beliefs, and ways of life reflect diverse identities that are challenged and perhaps even threatened—but that do not have to suffer extinction.

The Right to a Spiritual Heritage

Those who speak out in favor of indigenous peoples' rights include the right to maintaining a spiritual heritage. Many native groups maintain complex, detailed beliefs regarding the world around them. Some of these beliefs include the sacredness of certain places or objects and the importance of ancestors and burial grounds.

Indigenous Maya from the Mexican state of Chiapas march for peace.

TIMELINE

Late 1830s	1880s–1920s	1910–1970
Approximately 15,000 Cherokee march along what is later known as the Trail of Tears. Approximately 4,000 die.	Boarding schools across the United States aim to assimilate Native American students into mainstream white culture.	Australian officials remove approximately 100,000 Aboriginal children from their homes and families.

2004	2004	2005
UNICEF reports that discrimination frequently leads to crises of self-esteem and identity among indigenous populations.	More than 24 percent of Native Americans are described as living below the poverty line.	Juan Evo Morales Ayma is elected Bolivia's first indigenous head of state on December 18.

1992

Rigoberta Menchú Tum, who is of Mayan descent, is honored with the Nobel Peace Prize.

1994

In December, the UN declares August 9 International Day of the World's Indigenous People.

1997–2005

Government officials in Botswana force thousands of African Bushmen off their ancestral lands in the CKGR.

2006

Approximately 370 million indigenous peoples are residing in an estimated 90 countries all over the world.

2006

A US report reveals that several Native American children are hesitant to learn tribal languages because they want to appear "less Indian."

2006

Botswana's High Court rules that the eviction of the Bushmen from the CKGR was "unlawful" and "unconstitutional."

TIMELINE

2007

On September 13, the UN General Assembly adopts the United Nations Declaration on the Rights of Indigenous Peoples.

2008

In February, Australian Prime Minister Kevin Rudd formally apologizes to Aboriginal members of the "stolen generations."

2008

President Ian Khama of Botswana declares it impractical for the Bushmen to continue pursuing their traditional lifestyle as hunter-gatherers.

2009

The Bolivian government adopts a new constitution that offers that country's indigenous groups greater opportunities for autonomy.

2009

CNN reports that about 80 percent of the Lakota on the Cheyenne River Reservation in South Dakota are unemployed.

2008

Economic reports indicate that consumers have spent approximately $4 billion on fair trade–certified products.

2008

In Bogotá, Colombia, demonstrations organized by local indigenous peoples result in violent clashes with the police and military.

2008

In December, INAC reports a lower quality of life for local indigenous populations than what is considered the general average.

2009

In October, Chilean Mapuche report that police have begun attacking their children with pellets and tear gas.

2009

Experts estimate there are 827 fair trade–certified producer organizations across the globe.

2011

A court decision in Botswana declares that the Bushmen living in the CKGR do not have the right to access the reserve's water holes.

Essential Facts

At Issue

❖ As of 2006, approximately 370 million indigenous peoples resided in an estimated 90 countries all over the world. Many of these cultures date back thousands of years and existed prior to colonization or annexation by foreign powers. Today, however, a large number of indigenous populations face discrimination and economic disadvantage. Several are threatened with the loss of their lands and ways of life.

❖ Some indigenous groups prefer to practice either full autonomy or a partial measure of it. They often feel underrepresented or mistreated by mainstream governments and political systems. However, not everyone agrees with or accepts indigenous peoples' rights to self-determination.

❖ Indigenous populations continue to face a great deal of cultural discrimination that can take many shapes, ranging from overt violence to more subtle forms of prejudice. Many have been urged to abandon their languages, lands, and traditions and assimilate into mainstream society. This poses a threat to the preservation of indigenous peoples' cultural identities.

❖ Indigenous communities are often deeply impacted by poverty. Many are forced to seek income as migratory laborers or sweatshop workers. Such people generally have few rights and earn meager wages. As a result of these and other circumstances, indigenous groups tend to be challenged by economic disadvantage and, consequently, reduced standards of physical and mental health.

❖ Some experts believe that fair trade is a solution to many indigenous peoples' problems. This market approach is designed to help producers in developing countries achieve greater economic stability. It also typically promotes social awareness, workers' rights, and respect for the environment. Opponents of fair trade argue that, because it guarantees that retailers pay producers above-market prices, it discourages a competitive economy. In addition, they insist that it fails to aid the world's poorest indigenous populations.

CRITICAL DATES

1994

In December, the UN raised awareness for indigenous peoples by announcing that every year, August 9 will be used to celebrate International Day of the World's Indigenous People.

2004

UNICEF highlighted psychological effects of discrimination among indigenous groups. UNICEF reported that discrimination frequently leads to crises of self-esteem and identity among indigenous populations, prompting higher rates of alcoholism, substance abuse, depression, and suicide.

2007

The UN General Assembly adopted the United Nations Declaration on the Rights of Indigenous Peoples on September 13. This document consists of 46 articles that describe various privileges indigenous groups should not be denied.

2008

As fair trade became a more common practice, economic research showed that people around the world had spent approximately $4 billion on foods and wares that were certified as products of fair trade. Debate continues about the actual benefits of fair trade.

QUOTES

"I feel caged. My father taught me to hunt with a bow and arrow. We slept in the veld [open grasslands]—it was so free. But that has all been taken away, we can never go back."—*African Bushman Monto Masako*

"Poverty casts its darkest shadows upon indigenous people."—*Boutros Boutros-Ghali, former secretary-general of the United Nations*

Glossary

annexed
Conquered or taken over, as in territory.

assimilate
To blend into or adopt the customs of mainstream society.

autonomy
Political independence that often takes the form of self-government.

colonized
Settled by a foreign power.

commodities
Goods such as oil, grain, or gold that vary only slightly between producers.

conquistadores
Those who conquered portions of the Americas for Spain in the sixteenth century.

cooperatives
Associations whose members are typically independent farmers or manufacturers who work together as a larger business group to further their economic and social goals.

developing nations
Countries that are characterized by government, agricultural, economic, and industrial systems that are not fully established; these nations are often deeply affected by poverty.

dialects
Variations of a spoken language that are used in a particular region or culture.

discrimination
The act of treating someone differently or unfairly.

heritage
A collection of practices and traditions that are handed down from one generation to the next.

intermediary
In-between or serving as a middleman.

linguists
Scientists who study languages.

mainstream
Common or dominant beliefs and practices within a society.

migratory
Moving from place to place in search of work or seasonal labor.

moral code
A set of principles that address what is right and what is wrong.

poverty line
The minimal income that is needed to maintain a basic standard of living within a particular country; families who earn less than this figure are said to be poor.

prejudice
Discrimination that arises when someone judges another person.

reservation
Land set aside—often by a government body—for use by a particular person or group of people.

sweatshop
Related to factory labor that typically features substandard wages, long hours, and dangerous or extremely taxing working conditions.

ADDITIONAL RESOURCES

SELECTED BIBLIOGRAPHY

Blaser, Mario, Harvey A. Feit, and Glenn McRae, eds. *In the Way of Development: Indigenous Peoples, Life Projects, and Globalization*. New York: Palgrave Macmillan, 2004. Print.

Coates, Kenneth. *A Global History of Indigenous Peoples: Struggle and Survival*. New York: Palgrave Macmillan, 2004. Print.

Hall, Thomas D., and James V. Fenelon. *Indigenous Peoples and Globalization: Resistance and Revitalization*. Boulder, CO: Paradigm, 2009. Print.

Perkins, John. *Confessions of an Economic Hit Man*. San Francisco, CA: Berrett-Koehler, 2004. Print.

FURTHER READINGS

Burgan, Michael. *The Lakota*. New York: Marshall Cavendish Benchmark, 2007. Print.

Legay, Gilbert. *Dictionary of American Indians and Other Indigenous Peoples*. Hauppauge, NY: Barron's, 2007. Print.

Marcovitz, Hal. *Fair Trade*. Edina, MN: Abdo, 2011. Print.

Web Links

To learn more about indigenous peoples' rights, visit ABDO Publishing Company online at **www.abdopublishing.com**. Web sites about indigenous peoples' rights are featured on our Book Links page. These links are routinely monitored and updated to provide the most current information available.

For More Information

For more information on this subject, contact or visit the following organizations:

Center for World Indigenous Studies
PMB 214, 1001 Cooper Point Road SW Suite 140, Olympia, WA 98502–1107
360-586-5183
www.cwis.org
This organization conducts research related to the social, political, and economic issues that impact indigenous peoples.

Cultural Survival
215 Prospect Street Cambridge, MA 02139
617-441-5400
www.culturalsurvival.org
Cultural Survival partners with and works on behalf of indigenous peoples through campaigns and other efforts to promote their survival.

Fairtrade International
Bonner Talweg 177, 53129 Bonn, Germany
+49–228–949230
www.fairtrade.net
This contact can be used to obtain the latest data and statistics on fair trade and certification processes.

Source Notes

Chapter 1. Life on a Lakota Reservation

1. John King. "King: Life is bare bones on the Lakota reservation." *CNNPolitics.com*. Cable News Network, 13 Sept. 2009. Web. 22 Nov. 2009.

2. John King. "King: Life is bare bones on the Lakota reservation." *CNNPolitics.com*. Cable News Network, 13 Sept. 2009. Web. 22 Nov. 2009.

3. John King. "King: Life is bare bones on the Lakota reservation." *CNNPolitics.com*. Cable News Network, 13 Sept. 2009. Web. 22 Nov. 2009.

4. "International Day of the World's Indigenous People." *The Global Development Research Center*. N.p., n.d. Web. 22 Nov. 2009.

Chapter 2. From Southern Africa to India

1. "Namibia: 'Bushmen' face lifestyle threat." *African Conservation Foundation*. N.p., 14 Oct. 2007. Web. 24 Nov. 2009.

2. Andy McSmith and Christopher Finn. "Australia's stolen generation: 'To the mothers and the fathers, the brothers and the sisters, we say sorry.'" *The Independent*. Independent.co.uk, 13 Feb. 2008. Web. 24 Nov. 2009.

3. Andy McSmith and Christopher Finn. "Australia's stolen generation: 'To the mothers and the fathers, the brothers and the sisters, we say sorry.'" *The Independent*. Independent.co.uk, 13 Feb. 2008. Web. 24 Nov. 2009.

4. C.R. Bijoy. "The Adivasis of India: A History of Discrimination, Conflict, and Resistance." *People's Union for Civil Liberties*. N.p., Feb. 2003. Web. 24 Nov. 2009.

Chapter 3. Indigenous Peoples of the Americas

1. Milagros Salazar. "Peru: Indigenous People, Ignored Even by the Statistics." *IPS*. IPS—Inter Press Service, 10 Oct 2006. Web. 13 Dec. 2009.

2. "Rigoberta Menchú Tum." *Nobel Women's Initiative*. N.p., n.d. Web. 13 Dec. 2009.

3. "Speaking Out." *Smithsonian Institution, National Museum of Natural History, Department of Anthropology*. N.p., n.d. Web. 13 Dec. 2009.

4. James C Cobb. *Georgia Odyssey*. Athens, GA: University of Georgia Press, 2008. 12.

5. "Overcoming Prejudice." *Indian and Northern Affairs Canada*. N.p., n.d. Web. 13 Dec. 2009.

Chapter 4. Perspectives on Political Independence

1. Francisco López Bárcenas. "Indigenous Movements in the Americas: From Demand for Recognition to Building Autonomies." *Americas Program*. Fluxxus Digital Limited, 27 Feb. 2008. Web. 10 Feb. 2011.

2. Martin Garat. "Indigenous Autonomy: Anhelo Come True." *Indigenous Peoples Issues & Resources*. N.p., 2 May 2009. Web. 13 Dec. 2009.

3. "Aboriginal self-determination and autonomy." *Creative Spirits*. Creative Spirits, Jens-Uwe Korff, n.d. Web. 13 Dec. 2009.

4. Helda Martínez and Constanza Vieira. "Colombia: Brutal Crackdown on Indigenous Protest." *IPS*. IPS—Inter Press Service, 16 Oct. 2008. Web. 13 Dec. 2009.

5. Martin Garat. "Indigenous Autonomy: Anhelo Come True." *Indigenous Peoples Issues & Resources*. N.p., 2 May 2009. Web. 13 Dec. 2009.

SOURCE NOTES CONTINUED

Chapter 5. Struggling for Cultural Survival

1. Petri Hottola, ed. *Tourism Strategies and Local Responses in Southern Africa*. Cambridge, MA: CABI, 2009. 58.

2. "Eviction of Bushmen 'unlawful and unconstitutional.'" *Survival*. Survival International, 1969–2011, 5 Sept. 2006. Web. 13 Dec. 2009.

3. "President tells Bushmen their way of life is an 'archaic fantasy.'" *Survival*. Survival International, 1969–2011, 12 Dec. 2008. Web. 13 Dec. 2009.

4. "Racism in Aboriginal Australia." *Creative Spirits*. Creative Spirits, Jens-Uwe Korff, n.d. Web. 13 Dec. 2009.

5. Rod McGuirk. "Amnesty boss urges equality for poor Aborigines." *The Seattle Times*. The Seattle Times Company, 17 Nov. 2009. Web. 13 Dec. 2009.

6. Carolyn J. Marr. "Assimilation Through Education: Indian Boarding Schools in the Pacific Northwest." *University of Washington*. University of Washington Libraries, n.d. Web. 13 Dec. 2009.

7. Carolyn J. Marr. "Assimilation Through Education: Indian Boarding Schools in the Pacific Northwest." *University of Washington*. University of Washington Libraries, n.d. Web. 13 Dec. 2009.

8. Carolyn J. Marr. "Assimilation Through Education: Indian Boarding Schools in the Pacific Northwest." *University of Washington*. University of Washington Libraries, n.d. Web. 13 Dec. 2009.

9. Luz A. Murillo and Patrick H. Smith. "Cultural Diversity: Why It Matters in Schools and What Teachers Need to Know." *The University of Texas at Brownsville*. N.p., 10 Jan. 2007. Web. 13 Dec. 2009.

Chapter 6. Plagued by Poverty

1. "The Faces of Poverty." *United Nations*. United Nations Department of Public Information, Mar. 1996. Web. 13 Dec. 2009.

2. Ganesh Devy. "Development through Adivasi eyes." Association for India's Development. *AID Publications*, n.d. Web. 13 Dec. 2009.

Chapter 7. Searching for Solutions through Fair Trade

1. Elizabeth Weise. "Fair trade sweetens pot." *USA Today*. USA Today, 8 Feb. 2005. Web. 13 Dec. 2009.

2. Maricel Drazer. "Argentina: Fair Prices for Indigenous Crafts." *IPS*. IPS–Inter Press Service, 24 May 2006. Web. 13 Dec. 2009.

3. Elizabeth Weise. "Fair trade sweetens pot." *USA Today*. USA Today, 8 Feb. 2005. Web. 13 Dec. 2009.

Chapter 8. Mixed Views on Fair Trade

1. "Fair Trade Cocoa Cooperatives." *Global Exchange*. Global Exchange, 10 Nov. 2009. Web. 13 Dec. 2009.

2. Rebecca Smithers. "Fair trade branded 'unfair.'" *Guardian. co.uk*. Guardian News and Media Limited, 25 Feb. 2008. Web. 13 Dec. 2009.

3. Brendan O'Neill. "How fair is Fairtrade?" *BBC News*. BBC, 7 March 2007. Web. 13 Dec. 2009.

4. Brendan O'Neill. "How fair is Fairtrade?" *BBC News*. BBC, 7 March 2007. Web. 13 Dec. 2009.

Chapter 9. Other Efforts to Preserve Indigenous Cultures

1. "United Nations Declaration on the Rights of Indigenous Peoples." *United Nations*. N.p., 13 Sept. 2007. Web. 13 Dec. 2009.

2. "United Nations Declaration on the Rights of Indigenous Peoples." *United Nations*. N.p., 13 Sept. 2007. Web. 13 Dec. 2009.

3. "United Nations Declaration on the Rights of Indigenous Peoples." *United Nations*. N.p., 13 Sept. 2007. Web. 13 Dec. 2009.

4. "United Nations Declaration on the Rights of Indigenous Peoples." *United Nations*. N.p., 13 Sept. 2007. Web. 13 Dec. 2009.

5. "Aboriginal Politics & media." *Creative Spirits*. Creative Spirits, Jens-Uwe Korff, n.d. Web. 13 Dec. 2009.

6. Lucia Van Der Post. "Kalahari Bushmen: Crushed between Two Worlds." *New Heaven New Earth*. NewHeavenNewEarth, 19 Sept. 2009. Web. 13 Dec. 2009.

Index

About the Author

Katie Marsico is the author of more than 50 children's reference books. She worked for several years as a managing editor before she began her career as a freelance writer. She currently lives near Chicago, Illinois, with her husband, daughter, and two sons.

Photo Credits